Ben Blanchet is a thirteen-year-old boy who has autism. He is a homeschooled student, with many unique interests and abilities…abilities he refers to as his superpowers!

Maybe Autism Is My Superpower

BEN BLANCHET

AUSTIN MACAULEY PUBLISHERS™
LONDON • CAMBRIDGE • NEW YORK • SHARJAH

Copyright © Ben Blanchet (2020)

Ordering Information:
Quantity sales: special discounts are available on quantity purchases by corporations, associations, and others. For details, contact the publisher at the address below.

Publisher's Cataloging-in-Publication data
Blanchet, Ben
Maybe Autism Is My Superpower

ISBN 9781645362616 (Paperback)
ISBN 9781643788043 (Hardback)
ISBN 9781645750307 (ePub e-book)

Library of Congress Control Number: 2020931026

www.austinmacauley.com/us

First Published (2020)
Austin Macauley Publishers LLC
40 Wall Street, 28th Floor
New York, NY 10005
USA

mail-usa@austinmacauley.com
+1 (646) 5125767

I am writing this book for autism awareness and for all the children with autism.

– Ben

Thank you to my family for knowing that my autism is a superpower. Thank you to my supporters, Lauren Marra (MG ABA), the Music Academy for Special Learners, Caffeine Academy, and Waves of Communication.

CONTENTS

Introduction

As I am writing the introduction to this book, I am beaming with hope that what is shared will create a new and exciting awareness about the incredible gifts children with autism are blessed with.

Ben is a 13-year-old boy who has autism and immune deficiency. For many reasons, including his vulnerable immune system, my husband and I decided that homeschool would be the best option for him. At five years old, when other children of his age were heading off to kindergarten, I was praying that I could teach him to string two words together, and maybe by some miracle, he would someday be able to speak in full sentences, read books, and write. It is now 8 years later, and my expectations are far surpassed. What Ben has taught me is that when the focus on children becomes more about their strengths than their weaknesses, more about their abilities than their disabilities, then their gifts will soar… gifts that Ben refers to as his "superpowers."

One homeschool day, I asked Ben to do a writing assignment on a topic of his choice. He wasn't feeling well that day and couldn't decide on a topic, so I suggested he write about something that feels good and makes him happy. We had recently seen a Marvel superhero movie, so I asked Ben if he wanted to write about the movie. He smiled and replied, "Yes, because maybe I am a superhero too." I then asked him how he is a superhero. His response was, "Maybe autism is my superpower." WOW!

Ben then went on to write pages about how he hears, feels, and thinks differently… which led me to ask him more questions… which, in turn, led to this book and a tool to share with people all around the world to help them shift their mindset to thinking… maybe autism is not a disability… MAYBE AUTISM IS A SUPERPOWER.

– Angela Blanchet

Question: "Ben, if you were to write about your autism, what would you say?"

Ben: "Maybe autism is my superpower!"

Question: "Ben, what do you think a superpower is?"

Ben: "It's what superheroes do. They climb walls, fly, shoot beams, and dodge danger. They defeat the bad guys. They protect, help, and feel proud."

Question: "How do you feel like a superhero?"

Ben: "My ears are a superpower. I hear things differently because everything around me is like a music note. Everything has a pitch. Some things bother me, and some things don't."

Question: "What pitches do you like?"

Ben: "I like the pitches in elevators. There is Otis, Schindler and Thyssenkrupp. They are my favorite. They have several pitches. The door to Otis opens in the 'F' note. The door to Schindler opens in the 'B' note. The door to Thyssenkrupp opens in the 'C' note.

"When we go in the car and you turn on the radio, some songs are okay, but some are not because of the pitch of the instruments or the voice of the singers. I like the sound of country music the best. I also really like jazz chords. When I hear chords play on the piano, I can tell what notes they have and also if they are major, minor, diminished, or augmented chords without looking at the keys. I can just hear it and memorize it. I also know what notes are being played on all instruments when I hear them, like guitars, flutes, and violins too.

"People always laugh and cry and talk in different keys. All of them are different and some bother me, but most are okay.

"I like the sound of cash registers. NCR and Datalogic scanners are my favorite. NCR scanners make the F/A/C/D/ note sound, and Datalogic scanners make the A/E/C/ note sound. I like NCR the best because it has more sounds. Target has NCR scanners. That is why I like to go there and use the self-checkout machines.

"I hear the train from our house. The beeping of the train is the 'B' note, but the whistle of the train is unknown. The sounds of bees and flies scare me because of the buzzing. The pitch is unknown, but it bothers my ears. Sometimes, dogs barking in the neighborhood and the fire alarm from the firehouse also bother my ears. Sometimes, I can cover my ears to help. Sometimes, I have to make a humming sound so that I don't hear it.

"My ears also hear alerts differently than other people. There are many different types of alerts on the iPhones. When people get a text message, if the phone is on 'telegraph,' the text alert is a 'B' note. Some people have their phones set to 'pulse,' which is in 'B' sharp and other people have their phones set to 'keys,' which plays the A note. IPhones that are set to the 'glass' alert are my favorite because I like the sound of the A note. I do not like the weather alerts that come to the phone because the E/F#/B is a scary tune to me. Sometimes, when those notes are played at the same time, it upsets me.

"I also like the sounds of some TV theme songs and commercials because they relax me. I love the theme song to 'Everybody Loves Raymond.' It is played in 'C' major. I also love the theme song to 'The King of Queens.' It is in 'B' major and is a funny song to me. The Lorimar medley is at the end of some TV shows, such as 'Full House.' It is also in 'C' major. It starts and ends with a 'C' note and is very relaxing. The LG commercial – 'Life Is Good' – is so calming too. The notes are D/E/F/D/E/C/high C. The T-Mobile commercial has only 'C' & 'E' notes – C/C/C/E/C. It is so calming. Also, the 2003 Warner Brother's TV at the end of shows, C/F/G/F, is also very relaxing to my ears. But, the best sounds are on American Public Television – the F/G/A/C/B/D/C. It's at the end of a PBS show. Also, I like the Nissan Commercial that is in the key of 'C.' It is only a 'C' and 'G' note, but it's one of my favorites.

"Some of the toys I play with have a music pitch to them. I like to play Simon Air. You have to remember the order of the lights. When the blue light flashes, it makes a low 'G' note sound. When the yellow light flashes, it has a 'C' note, the red light makes the 'E' note and the green light makes the high 'G' note. So, I can also play the game – Simon – with my ears and keeping my eyes closed.

"Inside our house, there are things that sound to me like a musical note. When the microwave in the kitchen beeps, it is in the 'C' note. The Oster oven makes the 'B' note sound. When our doorbell rings, it goes 'D note B note,' and when our home phone rings, it goes 'F note A note.'"

Ben's perfect pitch ability was apparent at a very young age, when my sister gave him a keyboard to play with. There was a song bank on it which Ben would listen to while he watched the keys light up as it played. He would take his little index finger and point to the keys as the lights moved up and down, as if he was scanning them while listening. It would only take a few times of listening to one song for him to memorize it. Shortly after realizing this ability, my father saw an article in the newspaper about a new music school for children with special needs – The Music Academy for Special Learners in Hauppauge, NY. They were beginning a piano program for children with special needs and autism. It wasn't long after enrolling Ben, that we learned what perfect pitch was and realized that his ears were able to identify any note on any instrument. Amazing! I will never forget the summer day when my daughter and I heard the musical medley that the ice cream truck plays. She asked if she could go outside and stop the truck to buy an ice cream. I took her outside and we waited for the truck to near our home, but this never happened. I then realized that there was no ice cream truck outside! Ben had memorized the medley by ear and was playing it on the keyboard, down in our basement! He was playing this tune EXACTLY like the truck plays it. He was only 4 years old. Ben's perfect pitch ability didn't stop with music. As Ben grew older and became more verbal, he would often say things to me like "Stop laughing in 'A' sharp" or "The microwave should stop beeping in the 'C' note." Everything in Ben's environment seems to have a musical pitch, and I'm sure he is not the only child with autism like this... far from it! Many children with autism have musical ability and a perfect pitch. What a fascinating way to hear the world around you. So, the next time you see a child with autism or special needs, covering their ears or humming to drown out the noise around them, remember this... this is not part of their 'disability'... this is an amazing ability, and according to Ben, one of their superpowers!

Superpower 2 – A Super Memory

Question: "What is another way your autism makes you feel like a superhero?"

Ben: "I can remember things."

Question: "How do you remember things?"

Ben: "I'm not sure, I just do... I guess that's why it's a 'superpower.'"

Question: "What types of things do you remember?"

Ben: "I know where we are when you or Dad are driving me in the car by looking at the stores. I also know the names of the grocery stores in many of the different towns."

Question: "Wow, Ben, that's really cool! Can you give me some examples?"

Ben: "Sure. When I see the Uncle Giuseppe's from Northern State Parkway, I know we are in Melville, NY. When I see the Target from the Long Island Expressway, I know we are passing Henry Street in Commack, NY. When I hear about the store Publix, I know those people must live in Florida or Georgia. When I hear about Tesco, I know those people must be from the U.K. I also know that Safeway is in Washington and Alaska. I also know that Keyfood in Kings Park, NY, used to be Foodtown. Best Market in Syosset, Long Island, used to be King Kullen. King Kullen closed in 2017, and Best Market opened in 2018. Whole Foods will be opening at the former King Kullen in Commack, NY, expected date: April 3, 2019. Whole Foods only has 4 locations on Long Island, including Commack. Borders filed for bankruptcy and closed all if its stores in 2011. I miss it. Sears officially filed for bankruptcy in 2018. Toys 'R' Us filed for bankruptcy and closed all of its American stores in 2018. Lucky for Canada, they still have Toys 'R' Us. Toys 'R' Us was my childhood."

Ben's fascination with stores, and interest in reading and learning about store locations began at around 5 years old. I'm not sure what triggered this interest. I simply knew it existed. Whenever we would drive by a store that had closed down, he would tell me the date it closed on, as well as what was replacing it. I remember when Borders bookstore near us closed down. I asked Ben if he thought there were any other Borders bookstores in the world. He responded, "Yes, let me tell you about the rise, fall, and rebirth of Borders in Asia."

When Toys "R" Us went out of business in 2018, I found an obituary to the store in the notes in Ben's iPhone that read,

"RIP Toys 'R' Us 1957–2018, Kids like Toys 'R' Us, but in the next week they will close all of its stores because it filed for bankruptcy last September. I used to go to Toys 'R' Us with my family and I enjoyed it. Toys 'R' Us and Babies 'R' Us in Commack, NY will announce closure dates for the second time."

Ben: "One day, I went to the phone store with my mom to upgrade my phone from iPhone 6 to an iPhone X. I was excited, but we had to wait a long time in the store. Other people were in the store and asking each other questions that I just knew the answers to, so I started answering the questions, and they kept asking me more questions. When I heard a man ask what Wendy's fast food restaurant originally was, I knew it was Roy Rogers, so I told him. One man asked me if I knew who was buying the Best Market stores, and I knew it was Lidl. He also asked me if I knew the country Lidl was from, and I knew it was Germany. Other people in the store didn't know this. Sometimes, I'm surprised that people do not know these answers, but I do. It's probably my superpower.

"Another time I was surprised that people don't know the answers was when I was playing with kids over the summer. I was playing in the pool with other kids, last summer, and we started playing a trivia game and asked each other questions. Kids were asking questions about video games and foods. We had to pick A, B, or C. When I asked my questions, the kids didn't know the answers."

Question: "What questions did you ask the other kids?"

Ben: "One question I asked was 'What was 50 Route III in Smithtown, NY, originally a part of?' My choices were A. Fairfield Property B. Federal Realty or C. NAI Long Island. The answer was A. Fairfield Property.

"The other question I asked when it was my turn was, 'Where was the first Babies "R" Us Location? A. Commack, NY B. Massapequa, NY or C. Westbury, NY.' The answer was C. Westbury, NY.

"I remember my sister Lily say, 'How does Ben know all of this and what is he even talking about?' and I know it is just my superpower that I know things that a lot of people don't."

Recently, Ben's grandfather had to make an appointment to see an ophthalmologist. Ben had overheard the telephone conversation that was held when his grandfather called to tell me the date and time of his appointment. When I got off the telephone, Ben said to me, "Make sure Pop Pop knows his eye doctor appointment is in the 260 Middle Country Road Building."

He followed this by telling me the suite number. When I asked Ben how he knew this information, he stated, "From the directory… I have been in that building before and I memorized it."

Question: "Ben, I realize that you like to look at directories at office buildings, do you like to look at other maps as well?"

Ben: "I love to look at directories at medical office buildings and malls, and I also like to look at Google Maps. I can memorize them. I look at the apartment buildings, stores, shopping malls, and hospitals. It's easy to use Google Maps. You just scroll, zoom, and/or search. I can zoom and search very fast on Google Maps. It must be a superpower."

Question: "What are some things you look at and memorize from Google Maps?"

Ben: "I like to look at the North Shore Towers in Lake Success, NY, because it has so many amenities, such as: a fitness center, an indoor and outdoor pool, a golf course, two grocery stores, a restaurant, a pharmacy, and a branch of Chase Bank. It has a penthouse which has four bedrooms and more than three bathrooms, which is awesome! The North Shore Towers have 31 floors! That is so high! I also look at LeFrak City in Corona, Queens. It is off the Long Island Expressway, 495 West. It has sport courts, including a basketball court, tennis court, table tennis court, a soccer field, and a pool too. It looks like a lot of fun. I also look at apartments on Gerard Street in Huntington, NY. They have two realtors and are in walking distance to a Stop & Shop and the AMC movie theatre. To travel to Gerard Street from my home, all you have to do is take First Avenue to Pulaski Road, to Fort Salonga Road, and you make a right on New York Avenue and choose a parking spot. I also like to look at NYC on Google Maps because I love tall buildings. My favorite is the Empire State Building. I also love the One World Trade Center because it is the tallest building in New York City. There are some Whole Foods stores in NYC which are one of my favorite grocery stores."

Ben has had an interest in maps for as long as I can remember. I realized his keen sense of direction when he was seven years old. Like many children with autism, Ben would often wander. Because of this, he had a therapy dog and would wear a GPS tracking device. One day, I was alerted by his dog that he was nearing the front door. I followed him as he opened the door, stepped outside, and began to walk down the street. I, of course, quickly stopped him and asked, "Where do you think you are going?"

His response was "Chuck E Cheese." Ben did not have much language at this time, but when I asked him "How will you get there?" He answered, "Indian Head Road" and "Jericho." These were the exact roads that led to Chuck E Cheese. That was a huge awareness moment for me. I realized that, although Ben was so quiet when we drove around in the car and had little to no conversational speech ability, he was taking it all in. He was quiet, but he was aware, and apparently, he knew exactly where he was. The message here is that even when children with special needs are non-verbal or have little to no language, this does not mean they aren't aware of their surroundings, and it definitely does not mean that they are not learning or absorbing information! Limited speech does not mean a limited mind!

Question: "Can you tell me about some other things you are easily able to memorize?"

Ben: "I like to read a lot about health, and I like to watch videos online about health. I can memorize a lot about health and laboratory procedures."

Question: "Can you share with me a few things you have memorized about health?"

Ben: "I know there is a thing called 'antibiotic resistance' which is when you take too much antibiotics and they don't work anymore, and that can be dangerous. There are also superbugs that are antibiotic resistant bacteria that are difficult to treat. This is also dangerous. Also, it's important to know that the incubation period of a disease happens before you are sick, so you would still be contagious at this time. So, people should always wash their hands and cover their mouths when they cough or sneeze.

"I also know that substance abuse can be a big problem. This is when people take drugs when they are not sick. They can be prescription or illegal drugs. Nicotine is one of the hardest addictions for people to break. The best way to break that addiction is to never start in the first place. Some people smoke e-cigarettes to help them stop smoking but some e-liquids have cancer causing chemicals and heavy metals, including lead. Chewing tobacco isn't much better. It also contains nicotine, plus an added risk of mouth cancer. Drinking too much alcohol is also a problem for your health. Sometimes people drink irresponsibly. Alcohol messes up your thinking and motor skills. That's why it is dangerous to drink and drive. Alcohol acts as a depressant in the body, which is the opposite of a stimulant, so it makes you feel sleepy and numb.

"High blood pressure is sometimes a chronic health problem. It is caused by eating fatty and salty foods, and nicotine use. High blood pressure can cause heart problems and stroke. Diabetes can also cause the same problems and also blindness, kidney problems, and circulation problems. So, it is important to keep your blood sugar in good control by eating healthy, not eating too many sweets, and exercising.

"HIV and some types of cancers weaken the immune system. Acute lymphoblastic leukemia is the most common form of childhood cancer. Chronic leukemia is the opposite of acute. It has the same symptoms but is longer lasting. Sometimes, cancer spreads to other parts of the body. This is called metastases. Sometimes, chemotherapy, which is used to treat cancers, can damage the good cells in your body too.

"It is important for the body to get eight hours of sleep so that your immune system doesn't get weak. There are two types of sleep: NREM and REM. People dream during REM sleep.

"I know that doctors and lab technicians should always take universal precautions. This is when doctors wear gloves and masks and use complete protection. Nitrile gloves are my favorite because, in my opinion, they are more protective. Also, when you get your blood drawn, the phlebotomist should take a shallow approach to the vein. If the phlebotomy tube has a red top, it is a serum test, a tiger top is an SST – Serum Separation Test – a lavender top is for a CBC – Complete Blood Count. There is an order of blood draw which is important for a phlebotomist to follow. It tells them which tubes they should draw first and which tubes they should draw last. Red tops should be drawn first, then tiger tops, then lavender tops for a CBC. After blood is drawn, it is inverted and taken to the lab. It is inverted so that it doesn't clot. Sometimes, the tubes are put into a centrifuge for inverting. In my opinion, butterfly needles are the best because they are smaller. They are 23-25 gauge. Straight needles are 21-22 gauge which is bigger and can hurt more. Putting lidocaine cream on the arm before a blood test can help the blood draw not hurt so much."

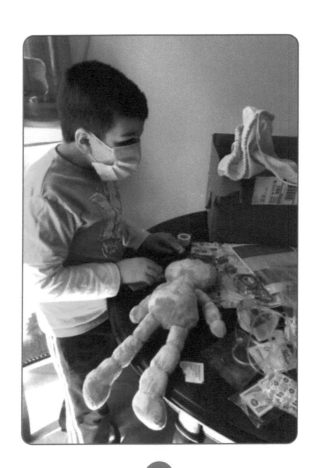

Because of Ben's immunodeficiency, he required frequent trips to the doctor's office and laboratory for blood tests. In order to desensitize him to this, we would have him watch videos of children going to the doctor and lab and read social stories to him. This quickly turned into more than in interest for Ben. It became a fascination and obsession for him to learn as much as he could about health. While other boys his age may have been interested in playing sports, Ben preferred to be watching online educational health videos.

When most 9 year old boys are asking Santa for toys and video games, Ben had something different in mind. I clearly remember at 9 years old, Ben sat on Santa's lap and with all his hope and desire asked, "Please, Santa please, can I get a phlebotomy training kit this year"? I believe that for the first time, Santa was dumbfounded! This was a request he has never had from a child, but this was also a request from the mind of child he had never encountered, the very special and unique mind of autism!

When Ben was 11 years old, he was admitted to the hospital. A nurse came into the room to draw his blood. I remember the shock on the nurse's face when Ben said to her, *"I have small veins so you may want to use a 23 or 25 gauge needle."*

I also remember when Ben was 12 years old, he was at the lab for a blood test. He asked the phlebotomist, *"Please, don't wipe the alcohol. It's better to let it air dry, and please, stop re-palpating my vein. It increases the risk of infection."*

The phlebotomist replied, "Wow, for a young boy, you sure do know a lot about phlebotomy."

Ben: "One time my mom and dad had to take me to the dermatology office because we didn't know if spots I had on my body were being caused by a virus or bacteria. I knew when the doctor was talking to my parents about doing a biopsy that it was going to be a punch biopsy. I knew this because I had listened about punch biopsy on YouTube. So, I asked the doctor, 'Will you be doing a punch biopsy, yes or no?'

"When she said 'Yes,' I knew it was because I had a deeper skin lesion, and punch biopsies are used for deeper skin lesions like moles or warts. A punch biopsy is like a cookie cutter. I also knew that this meant I would need stiches and I was scared. I reminded them to please take universal precautions and wear gloves. The doctor used a punch and syringe and needle for the lidocaine injection. I asked for dissolvable stitches so I would not have to come back again. I was happy when it was over."

What Ben is writing about may seem like random memorized facts – which they are – but it shows the gift of a special mind. One that not only reads or listens to information, but also absorbs it like a sponge. If you haven't already noticed, many children on the autism spectrum have the ability to memorize information… whether it is facts about presidents, makes and models of cars, or health facts about the human body. This is far from a disability. This is an amazing ability that many 'neuro typical' people struggle with. So, the next time you hear a child with special needs talking off topic with what seems like random, useless facts, consider the amazing potential and use for this special superpower. For they will make incredible researchers, doctors, and lawyers. Do not dismiss these conversations. Engage them with wonderment and fascination.

Superpower 3 – A Heightened Awareness

Question: "Are there any other superpowers that you have that you want to share in this book?"

Ben: "Yes, I notice things that you and Dad, and Lily do not notice."

Question: "What types of things do you notice?"

Ben: "I notice when two things are similar in two different places that we go to, and that is why I can remember them. Like, I notice that the elevator in Lake George at the Fort William Henry Hotel is the same as the elevator at Spring Hills Suites in Hershey Park. They are both Schindler elevators. I also notice that the scanners in Target are the same as the scanners in Trader Joe's. They are both NCR scanners. I also notice that Walmart and Stop & Shop both have Stanley automatic doors, and Keyfood and Target both have a T53 Tomra RVM – Reverse Vending Machine. I notice them, and I hear them, and I remember them."

Question: "Wow, Ben, this is interesting information. I know how much you like elevators and scanners, but I didn't realize you knew about reverse vending machines and automatic doors. Can you tell me more about that?"

Ben: "Sure. There are three brands of automatic doors that I like. I like Horton, Besam, and Stanley. Target has Besam doors. Walmart and Stop & Shop have Stanley doors. Besam are my favorite automatic doors because they have more decals. All brands of automatic doors have decals that say, 'In/Out/Do Not Enter/Caution,' but Besam has 3 versions of the 'Do Not Enter' sign and I like the options. I also like returning bottles and cans for money at RVM machines – reverse vending machines – at the grocery stores. Some models only take one material and other models take all three materials – plastic, cans, and glass. The brands of RVM machines I like are Tomra and Envipco. I like Envipco the best because some models take more than one bottle at a time. The King Kullen, in Huntington Station, NY, has the Envipco Ultra 48 machine. This is a great machine *because* it takes all three materials, but it only takes one bottle at a time. The Best Market in East Northport, NY, has an RVM that takes all three bottles at one time. Some CF 1500 models of RVM also have coin dispensers on them. I like this a lot because you do not have to take a receipt to the register. King Kullen in Saint James, NY has a coin dispenser on their RVM, but that may no longer be, since King Kullen is being bought and replaced by Stop & Shop."

Question: "Thank you, for sharing these interesting facts. Is there any other type of equipment you want to talk about?"

Ben: "Yes, I love gaming systems. I have a lot of them. I have an Xbox 1, Xbox 360, PS3, PS Vita, Wii, Wii U, Nintendo DS, Nintendo DSI, and Nintendo 3DS. Being able to perform system transfers is another superpower I have. Sometimes, I like to play the games. Minecraft is my favorite. I love building my Minecraft world. It is very big. It has supermarkets, hospitals, apartment buildings, and other stores. I keep stores alive in Minecraft that have gone out of business, such as Borders, Sports Authority, and A & P grocery store. I have also created Best Hospital in my Minecraft world which is a hospital that offers free healthcare with no insurance required. Sometimes, instead of playing games, I like to do system transfers. First, I download the transfer. Next, I go into data transfer tools, and then I perform the system transfer. I choose what I want to transfer and '*voila*' it transfers."

Question: "I remember one time, your friend James came over to play video games with you and he became upset because he said you weren't playing the game, and he wasn't sure what you were doing. Do you remember that?"

Ben: "Yes, I was transferring data from Wii to the WiiU. He thought it was boring, but the Wii was outdated, and I thought it needed to be transferred. So, I had to enter the WiiU transfer tool setting to transfer data before we could play any games together."

When Ben was turning seven years old, he had a game truck birthday party. The game truck was equipped with many different gaming systems for Ben and his friends to play. During the party, I went into the truck to check on Ben and asked the gaming attendant if all was going well. The man looked at me, with a look of confusion, and said, "Well, all the children are playing games, but your son has been doing something else for the past hour." When I asked him what that something was, he replied, "He is in the setting menu and reconfiguring all of the set-ups." I wasn't surprised. This was a perfect birthday for Ben!

Superpower 4 – The Need to Read

Question: "Is there anything else that you notice because of your superpowers?"

Ben: "Yes! I notice and can remember signs on the buildings, like real estate signs, that we pass in the car."

Question: "Can you tell me about some signs that you remember?"

Ben: "Sure. The 2171 Jericho Turnpike Building has a Fairfield Property Sign. The 50 Hillside Village Plaza – also known as, 50 Route 111 Smithtown, NY – has a Damianos Realty Group sign. This is the same group on the sign as the 222 building on Jericho Turnpike, in Smithtown. The Huntington Square Mall used to have a NAI realty group sign but now has a Federal Realty sign, and the Melville Mall Plaza – where Uncle Giuseppe's is – has a Federal Realty Group sign. Veterans Memorial Plaza has a Kimco Realty sign.

"I also notice signs inside of buildings and can remember them too. In the pediatrician's office in Huntington, there is a *'How to Put a Baby to Sleep'* sign. It says that babies need to sleep alone in a safely approved crib. It says how to place a baby to sleep safely with no toys and no bottles. In the immunology office in Great Neck, there is a *'Cover Your Cough'* poster that reminds people to cover their mouths when they cough to prevent the spread of germs. It says, *'Clean your hands and cover your cough.'* At the endocrinologist at the 250 Middle Country Road building, there is a poster of the affiliates of hospitals. It says the hospital affiliates are Huntington Hospital, LIJ Hospital, North Shore University Hospital, and The Cohen's Children's Medical Center."

Although Ben's speech was quite delayed, he was hyperlexic and reading at very a young age. He would barely speak a word, but would read the signs in the supermarkets as I pushed him down the aisle in the shopping cart. As he grew older, and his interests became more specific about health and grocery stores, I would find him reading every poster in a medical office and noticing every detail on signs in grocery stores. He not only reads these signs, he stores them in his memory, indefinitely.

Question: "I notice that you read a lot of the signs in the medical office buildings. Do you like to read?"

Ben: "Yes, I do, especially about medical facts. I can also read really fast, faster than many people, which is another superpower I have."

Question: "How did you learn to read so quickly?"

Ben: "I didn't learn it. I can just read really fast when I use a highlighter or pencil. The scribbling helps me read very fast. It sometimes feels insane because the words move really quickly, but the highlighter and pencil help me. Also, when I focus, I can read very quickly on the computer and on ipad apps."

Very recently, after giving Ben a highlighter to help him visually keep track of where he is when reading, I noticed his speed reading ability. At first, I thought he was avoiding some reading assignments because it would look to me like he was scribbling or coloring over the words. But, soon after, I realized that with a pencil or highlighter in hand while he reads, something amazing happens. The speech at which he reads and processes becomes heightened, or, as Ben refers to it, 'insane.'

> It sometimes feels insane because the words move really quickly, but the highlighter and pencil help me.

Question: "Amazing Ben! You have many incredible superpowers. What do you plan on doing with these cool superpowers?"

Ben: "If I decided to, because of my special ears, I could give music lessons, tune instruments to make them on pitch or tell people the notes in songs. Because I can read fast, if I decided to, I could do speed research about health and medical topics because I like those topics. Because I know a lot about supermarkets and check-out machines, I want to open my own supermarket one day. It will be called 'Great American Supermarket.' I know my superpowers will help me."

There is unlimited potential for the unique and special strengths that children with autism have. The trick is to pay close attention to these strengths. Often times, we worry about children with special needs and the focus becomes more on their deficits and delays than their extraordinary skills. When our attention goes to how they are not 'typical,' we lose sight of their strengths and gifts. The world can use the great abilities these children have to offer. What a better, more interesting world it would be if we could all shift our mindset to see their superpowers.

Question: "Thank you for sharing all of this, Ben. How would you like to end this book? What else do you want people to know?"

Ben: "I want people to know that everybody has a superpower, even kids who don't have autism have superpowers, but I think kids with autism's superpowers are different and special. I am happy. I like having autism and I am excited about growing up and using my superpowers."